Poet

DILL

THE CRUISING AUK

GEORGE JOHNSTON

TORONTO   OXFORD

THE CRUISING AUK

UNIVERSITY   PRESS   1959

For Jeanne

Some of these poems have previously appeared in
The Atlantic Monthly, *The Canadian Forum*, *Contemporary
Verse*, *Fiddlehead*, *Harper's Magazine*, *Mayfair*,
The New Yorker, *Pan-ic*, *The Spectator*, and
The Tamarack Review. The poems 'War on the Periphery'
and 'Rapture', 'Roses' and 'O Earth, Turn!', and
'Ice at Last' are copyright (1951, 1955, and
1956 respectively) The New Yorker Magazine, Inc.

Second Impression 1959
Third Impression 1960

PRINTED IN ENGLAND BY
HAZELL WATSON AND VINEY LTD
AYLESBURY AND SLOUGH

Part One

THE POOL

Part Two

THE CRUISING AUK

Part Three

IN IT

Part One

THE POOL

THE POOL

A boy gazing in a pool
Is all profound; his eyes are cool
And he's as though unborn, he's gone;
He's the abyss he gazes on.

A man searches the pool in vain
For his profundity again;
He finds it neither there nor here
And all between is pride and fear.

His eyes are warm with love and death,
Time makes a measure of his breath;
The world is now profound and he
Fearful, on its periphery.

LOVE OF THE CITY

After a week of wandering through the world
Eating wherever we could, sleeping, washing ourselves
Wherever we could, in bars and railway rooms,
We came to this great city. Nothing
Will persuade us ever to leave it again.

The city loves us now it's moved us in:
The yellow sky comes down and fills the room;
Dirt on the floor is kind, the walls are kind,
Everyone's kind to us wherever we go.

And truly when death comes where will he find
A better room than here, better arrangements,
More courtesy, more eager friendliness
Than in this excellent street-scattered city,
This home, this network, this great roof of pity?

MOONLIGHT

Those of us who love the moon
   And pause to look at her
Turn our protected souls too soon
   Out of her naked air.

Yet up she comes across the sky
   Lenticular and still
Putting the secret darkness by
   On floor and window sill.

How does she look on us who now
   Leave her explicit light
Turning, with angel-guarded brow,
   Each to his private night?

NIGHT NOISES

Late at night in night's neglected places
The busy diesel shunter thumps and grinds
As to and fro he singles out and chases
The helpless cars whose businesses he minds.

He enters dreams in unexpected guises
Suggesting jungles, jungle laughter, screams,
Telephone calls, pursuits and wild surprises,
Desperate croquet games and froggy streams.

A noise of idling river water comes
Across the cindered yard that's his demesne
And qualifies his busy to's and from's,
Mumbling of spongy pastures, far and green.

A solitary streetcar, deep in town,
Pesters the late sky with electric sparks.
Behind a million windows Sleep, the clown,
Draws out his turn. The cats are in the parks.

AFTER THUNDER

In pools the city realigns itself
But wrong way to. There is a smell of earth,
A smell of thunder, still, in the ecstatic air
After the passion and flood of August rain.

These pleasures come by streetfuls, they
Come in excess, as though they didn't care,
And overwhelm us; they bear an edge of pain
Which pierces us.

The city now, washed by a summer shower,
Offers such overwhelming careless pleasure:
Pools on the pavement, creeks along the lane,
An air so sweet among the boughs and bricks
That only birds, who aren't afraid of gods
And have no language, give the time a voice
Which pierces us: the ecstatic edge of pain.

TIME IN A PUBLIC WARD

As life goes on to worse and worse
The bed beside me calls the nurse
And says, It's getting worse, I guess.
She makes the worse a little less
By needle. Soon along the wall
Another bed puts in a call.

After pills the lights go down;
The walls turn gray and pink and brown.
Time passes. All at once a jet
Of orange lights a cigarette
Within whose glow a caverned eye
Watches the cinder burn and die.

The walls go back to gray and pink
And brown again. One hears a sink
And low voices, rustling feet;
There's music somewhere, late and sweet.
Clocks in the town put by the night
Hour by hour, ticked and right.

WAR ON THE PERIPHERY

Around the battlements go by
Soldier men against the sky,
Violent lovers, husbands, sons,
Guarding my peaceful life with guns.

My pleasures, how discreet they are!
A little booze, a little car,
Two little children and a wife
Living a small suburban life.

My little children eat my heart;
At seven o'clock we kiss and part,
At seven o'clock we meet again;
They eat my heart and grow to men.

I watch their tenderness with fear
While on the battlements I hear
The violent, obedient ones
Guarding my family with guns.

KIND OFFICES

Andrew, an understanding boy,
Helps Cathleen; he gets her toy
Or puts her dolly in her hand;
He sits her up, he makes her stand;
He picks her dolly up again
And gives it back to her and then
Re-erects her on her feet.
In all he does his air is sweet,
Olympian, perhaps; his smile
Is heaven's blandest. She meanwhile
Is rage itself. I cannot tell
Her rage: she's brimstone pits and hell.

RAIN

Yellow lights in the dark
And streets weak with rain and men;
I'd rather never have been born
Than feel the way I do again.

I'd rather never see the light
Than see it through a window pane
On which I feel myself run down
In weakness, with the drops of rain.

REST HOUR

Noises coming down the stairs,
Thumping noises, bumping chairs,
Roaring, whistling, muscle testing
Tell the hour of Andrew's resting.

Giant in his moods and grace,
Giant blood and giant pace
He fills the hour after lunch
Fighting gods with heave and punch.

Grievous energies of growth,
Storms of pride and tides of sloth
Sweep across his giant soul
Against the gods, the small and whole,

In vain, heroically in vain;
Noises come downstairs again.
The gods lunge and leap away
Knowing they'll win, but not today.

CATHLEEN SWEEPING

The wind blows, and with a little broom
She sweeps against the cold clumsy sky.
She's three years old. What an enormous room
The world is that she sweeps, making fly
A little busy dust! And here am I
Watching her through the window in the gloom
Of this disconsolate spring morning, my
Thoughts as small and busy as her broom.

Do I believe in her? I cannot quite.
Beauty is more than my belief will bear.
I've had to borrow what I think is true:
Nothing stays put until I think it through.
Yet, watching her with her broom in the dark air
I give it up. Why should I doubt delight?

MONEY IN POCKET

I've got money in my pockets,
Excellent pockets because there's money in them;
I can't feel low while there's paper for my fingers
In my excellent pockets, Caesar's mark on it.

I've got children in my rooms,
Blood-borne hostages, arrows from my side:
I can't sleep heavy while they're breathing in their beds
Who burst through my passageways and grow me back to earth.

I've got time in my clocks
And beer in my cellar and spiders in my windows:
I can't spend time nor drink all the beer
And I feel in the spread web the spider's small eye.

THE LIFE IN AUGUST

The prospect is of ribbed clouds across the sky
And blue water when the air is clear and the weather fine all day;
Then when the rocks are hot the turtles doze
And at night frogs pontificate across the bay in sonorous dignity.

Islands are bent then when the wind is westerly,
And the sky stands in green-blue, blue-green
Over the everlasting swishing of the whitecaps.

CATS

i

Pussy's caught a baby bird
   And she's so pleased with it
She's purring as she's never purred;
   She lets it go a bit
As though she held it by a thread
Or love, perhaps. Above her head

The air's extravagant with grief.
   The season over all
Is prodigal of bone and leaf
   And feathers too; the fall
Scatters the birds and leaves at last.
Eat it, pussy, life flies past!

Every yard has a cat these days
  Watching, footing, blinking;
Every tree has a cheeky squirrel,
  Seemingly all unthinking,
  Going his squirrel ways
As though no cat in the world were waiting, slinking.

Life is exquisite when it's just
  Out of reach by a bound
Of filigree jaws and delicate paws
  That feel their points in the ground,
  That drop their drips in the dust . . .
Pounce! Up the tree again! The tails whip round.

FLIGHT

All day long the clouds go by,
Early winter clouds, not high;
Wide as charity they range,
Restless, regimented, strange.

From my neighbourhood a crow
Takes it in his head to go
Somewhere else he knows about;
Melancholy bird, no doubt.

Up he rises from a tree
Where a yellow leaf or three
Still hang on for hanging's sake,
Tug their yellow stems and shake.

Caw! he cries, as though he knew
Something worth his while to do
In an empty tree elsewhere;
Flap! he takes his blackness there.

Me too! I would like to fly
Somewhere else beneath the sky,
Happy though my choice may be
Empty tree for empty tree.

Part Two

THE CRUISING AUK

THE CRUISING AUK

Questioning Mr. Murple
I found that he agreed
—We all, in fact, agreed—
It was a splendid auk
Flying across the sky.

And such a pleasure it is to see an auk
Shadow the sun with his little wings and his beak,
Going about his business in the air
Or hurrying home, or merely taking the weather!

Surely his eye belittles our despair,
Our unheroic mornings, afternoons
Disconsolate in the echo-laden air—
Echoes of trumpet noises, horses' hooves.

Splendid, however, we can
Rejoice in him, cruising there:
He is our uncle and lo,
O Mr. Murple, O beloved friends,
Airborne!

IN THE POND

The pond in Mr. Murple's yard
  I feel it in my shoes;
Deep in my shoes I feel the pond
  In Mr. Murple's yard.

And how much wiser will I be
  When I am in the pond?
When over me the sky is wet
  Will I much wiser be?

A little bird beside the pond
  Angles his eye at me
Where very deep and very wet
  I lie, beneath the pond.

Well may the bird look down on me,
  Cocking his little eye;
He knows the way to Paradise
  But he doesn't know me.

A MYSTIC OF THE AIR AGE

As though to pass beyond herself
Mrs. McGonigle emplaned;
Behold her from her pantry shelf
Remote, poised in a speck, contained!

Speeding, speeding, ah behold
Mrs. McGonigle afar
In the intense inane and cold
Where disembodied spirits are!

Extreme is yonder stratosphere,
The uttermost and least of air,
And while our mortal clay is here
Mrs. McGonigle's is there.

ICE AT LAST

When ice at last has come across the pond
And the old angry sun dismissed himself
In roasted lobster colour;
When trees all bare divaricate their twigs
Against the salmon sky and then go black,
This is when the accomplished Mr. Murple
Splendid on skates comes forth to spin the night
Upon his arms outstretched and whirling eyeballs.

Coffee drinkers fill the hut with steam;
They warm themselves within against the cold
That creaks without and circumvents the light,
While Mr. Murple, in a cloud of frost
Centripetal,
Turns on his pivot skates the captive sky.

LIGHT LITERATURE

In the short sharp winter twilight
   When beans are in to cook
Edward under the trilight
   Reads a detective book.

He scares his inner workings
   Into a fluid state
And his outer same to jerkings
   And yet he sits up late

Reading of nervous habits
   And nervous ways to kill;
The suspects breed like rabbits
   Till all the rooms are still.

Then up he creeps to his attic
   Feeling his instincts near
As a radio feels its static
   And voices mixed and queer.

Life has ebbed to a flicker
   Of neon light in town;
The attic waits with a snicker
   To bed poor Edward down.

RAPTURE

Sweet lovers lie around the bay
Lapped in each other's arms:
Mrs. Beleek with Dr. Gay,
Joad with Miss Decharmes,
Snug in their cabins tucked away
Sleeping the early hours of day.

Fishes within the burnished bay
Dimple the face thereof
Leaping to enter, as they may,
The mirror world above.
Delicate fishes, how they play!
Rapture is in the air today.

FUN

Elaine sleeps in her maiden bed
Still as the moonlight overhead;
Dreaming, across the way from her
Mrs. McGonigle's boarders stir;
Innocent boarders' dreams are sweet
Of beauty sleeping across the street.

Only the innocent have fun:
The beautiful Elaine is one,
The boarders are another seven;
Never a thought they give to heaven
Until their innocence is through.
Ah then, sweet joy, sweet grief, adieu!

POOR EDWARD

Whose hat is moving on the water's face
Making toward the sea a doubtful pace?
Poor Edward's, I'm disconsolate to say.
He owed me twenty dollars, by the way.
I look along the darkening bank and wonder
How Edward and his wisdom came asunder.

The air grows cool, the crowd has partly gone;
The lights begin to fidget off and on;
The boats kechunk and creak as to and fro
And up and down and through the bridge they go
Fishing, fishing where the water's deep
For Edward and his trouble, sound asleep.

MUSIC ON THE WATER

Saturday night she comes in her little boat
When the air is warm on the smoky river, afloat,
Making her presence felt in her flickering oars:
A journeying wound between the fragile shores.

Nights of splendour she's been to splendid men,
Swallowed them whole and spit them up again,
After which they've forgotten her perhaps—
As though she might have remembered them, poor chaps.

Now they're distributed about the town,
Two in a meeting, one in a dressing gown,
One in a hospital bed with stinking bones,
One in a radio drama, making groans.

One is a kind, white-eyebrowed public man,
Used to write poems and at times still can;
Fame is his breakfast food and evening prayer;
Saturday night he dozes in his chair.

Out on the skin of water she sings a song,
Sweet but a little bit flat and sometimes wrong;
Under the bridge it wobbles as she goes by
And wastes away in the willow trees and the sky.

The song she sings is a Pentecostal hymn
According to which Earth's glories are rather dim
Whereas the rewards of the just are very bright;
Low kind of song, but it serves her turn all right.

QUEENS AND DUCHESSES

Miss Belaney's pleasure is vast,
    Indeed it fills the night;
She doesn't remember who kissed her last
    But he did it good, all right.

She doesn't remember who broke her flowers
    When her fastenings came undone;
Her lipstick hasn't been straight for hours,
    She's had a night of fun.

Around her head is a haze of gold,
    Pleasure shines in her dress
Illuminating its every fold,
    Blessing each drunken tress.

Queens, queens have been here before
    And left their crowns outside,
Lifted like moons across the floor
    Their bosoms deep and wide.

Queens, queens, they smile and go,
    Their loves and deaths are sad;
Duchesses now and again stoop low;
    Miss Belaney is bad.

HOME AGAIN

Home again at four o'clock and up the sleeping stair,
Darkness in my loving parts, serpents in my hair,
Having been a reigning moon for half the loving night
And then a piece of iced cake for any god to bite;
Now I am a bent doll, I shed my silky stuff
And soon I'll be a sleeping heart. The gods got enough.

ANNABELLE

Annabelle has yellow teeth
And solid rubber underneath,
Golden polish on her toes
And pink and purple underclothes.
Nothing effervesces quite
As Annabelle when she is tight.

39

ON THE PORCH

What's on your mind tonight,
   Mary bloody Jane?
Why do you click the light
   Laughing like a drain?
Gentlemen are a dying race,
   Click it on again!

It isn't the way you walk
   Drifting down the street,
It isn't the way you talk
   Doing things with your feet,
It isn't the way you friz your hair
   And make your odours sweet.

A fellow's not made of glass
   Nor he isn't made of steel,
Some of the time he's an ass
   Some of the time he's a heel
Some of the time he's a shot down god
   And that's the way I feel.

THE ROLL CALL

Names of my aunts in order: Mrs. Balls,
Mrs. McGonigle, Lou, old Great-aunt Hairy,
Gentle, unmentionable Aunt Beleek
Who's intricate in underwear and shoes,
Who's fickle in them, fiddled, fled, forgotten—
My sweetest aunt, Beleek, and slightly rotten.

The roll call comforts me. Bless Aunt McGonigle,
Bless Mrs. Balls,
Bless all my aunts! I name their splendid names,
My queens of air, my dolls,
And my mortality, alas!

Day light passes. Night light passes too,
And all my aunts, however full in sight,
However giant-bowelled, -breasted, -sinewed,
Will founder, as the suns behind the chimneys;
Nor even fickle Aunt Beleek will linger,
Singled out by the somewhat smelly finger
Of recollection, poking among the drawers.
How can my wormy shelves and cupboards keep her
That have so many wormy things to keep?

ELAINE IN A BIKINI

Mrs. McGonigle's boys enjoy the sun
By gogglesful, and stare along the beach
Whose innocence is almost all Elaine,
   Almost, but not quite, all.

Felicitously she comes in every eye
Bending her knees and tender finger nails
While the incalculable strings gather in
   What's hers to gather in.

Her feet entice themselves across the sands
Down to the water's edge, and the old sea
Fumbles about the naked afternoon
   As though in paradise.

I am felicitous too on the bright shore
Waiting for darkness with the roving boys
And all but gathered in myself with strings,
   What's mine to gather in.

ART AND LIFE

Sadie McGonigle, Mrs. McGonigle's daughter,
Is in a state of art from head to foot;
She's spent the afternoon with suds and water
And creams and mud; her lines and points are put
And every inch is tender to the view—
Elegant work of art and artist too.

Sweet love, that takes a master piece like this
And rumples it and tumbles it about,
Why can he not be happy with a kiss?
He turns the shimmering object inside out
And all for life, that's enemy to art.
Now where's your treasure, little scented heart?

THE QUEEN OF LOP

She works all day at a big machine that lops and lops and lops;
At five o'clock she does her face and the big machine it stops;
Home again on a public bus she goes to her little flat,
Cooks a chop and forgets the lop and the wash-up and all that.

The days go on as they always do and the evenings pass in fun;
Edward comes with his gloomy face, he makes the hours run;
Maybe they watch a picture show in the lovely dark abyss
And if Edward's good and the show is good it's the next best
                                     thing to bliss.

The wind that overcasts the lakes and wears across the hills
Rattles itself among the city's roofs and window sills;
Around her bed the noises come, they give her dreams a steer:
The little flat becomes a boat on the ocean dark and queer.

The big machine is aboard the boat and so is Edward's face;
The shores go back, the thunders come, Leviathan gives chase;
On and on through the dreadful hours the winds and waters run
Until the walls wake up again and the curtains catch the sun.

The waters ebb from the papered room, the air is filled with light;
Bacon smells and coffee smells begin the day's delight;
On to the public bus again and on to the big machine
Whose lop is a well-run kingdom, ruled by a decorous queen.

A SAINT

Around the corner, down the street,
I overtook and turned to greet,
Taking his troubles for a walk
My old friend Boom. We had a talk
And as it happened we agreed
On many things, but on the need
Especially of mental strife
And of a whole new source of life.
The evening shone like polished brass.
Alas, said mournful Boom, alas!
While all around the chickadees
Hunted for bugs among the trees.

Boom is a saint, his sufferings
Put him in the know of things,
Teach him what is what and what
In spiritual things is not.
And when he looks upon us all
His heart contracts into a ball
Which is the perfect form of grief;
Its perfectness provides relief.

Another kind of perfect form
Provides relief for Uncle Norm
But Uncle Norm is not a saint
And neither I suppose I ain't.

45

DUST

Old Mrs. McWhirter is musty dusty old;
Down she goes to her cellar, it's full of bugs and cold;
Up she goes to her bottles, they're pink and green and brown;
Everywhere is a hairpin, they're always coming down.

Out from her dusty nightgown her dusty angels creep;
They harp and sing in the twilight before she goes to sleep
Sweet notes on the staircase that go kaplink and fall
Among the dusty shadows from the cellarway and hall.

Nobody knows but the angels how deep the dark goes down;
They won't tell Mrs. McWhirter, they flash their wings and clown;
Mrs. McWhirter mutters, the angels tease and scold;
A glory comes from their feathers, their voices ring like gold.

Dear Mrs. McWhirter, I wish she wouldn't die
In the dusty way she's planned it: I wish the Lady Sky
Having come home from her orbits and interstellar space
Would set aside in Eternity somewhere a dusty place

Where Mrs. might spat with her angels as thoughts together spat
In the dome of Eternal Wisdom, under the Eternal Hat;
But her bugs and bottles and hairpins will have to stay behind
Because Eternity's stuffy and perhaps a bit unkind.

ROSES

Among the roses down behind the house
Snip snap snip! go the little cutting pliers;
Sweet Miss Knit, who is a kind of a mouse,
Is gathering buds and blooms for Mr. Byers.
Mr. Byers is a kind of a hungry cat
Whose hunger somehow isn't for sweet Miss Knit;
She loves his magnificent person, which is fat,
And longs to be devoured every bit.

Ah roses, roses on Mr. Byers' table
That lean your thorns above the polished wood!
Miss Knit would borrow your deaths if she were able
To darken her small heart, discreet and good.
And yet the room's mahogany-deep light
And all the little rainbows in the glass
Seem to surround her movements with delight
And watch her mouse's footsteps as they pass.

NOCTAMBULE

Mr. Murple's got a dog that's long
And underslung and sort of pointed wrong;
When daylight fades and evening lights come out
He takes him round the neighbour lawns about
To ease himself and leak against the trees
The which he does in drops and by degrees
Leaving his hoarded fluid only where
Three-legged ceremonious hairy care
Has been before and made a solemn sign.
Mythology, inscrutable, canine,
Makes his noctambulation eloquent
And gives a power of meaning to his scent
That all who come and sniff and add thereto
And scratch the turf, may know they have to do
With Mr. Murple's underslung long dog,
His mark, his manifesto and his log.

THE BULGE

Nobody knows what's growing in Bridget,
　　Nobody knows whose is, what's more:
Maybe a beauty queen, maybe a midget,
　　Maybe a braided bloke to stand by the door.

Lovely full Bridget, her eyes are like figs,
　　Her belly's an ocean, heaving with fish,
Her heart is a barnyard with chickens and pigs,
　　Her outside's a banquet, her tongue is a dish.

Something enormous is bulging in Bridget—
　　A milkman, a postman, a sugar-stick, a slop,
An old maid, a bad maid, a doughhead, a fidget.
　　Multiple sweet Bridget, what will she drop?

THE ALDERMAN'S DAY IN THE CITY

Down in the tar-warm city
The little children play,
They wig and wag with their faces
Among the bricks all day.

Up at his desk the alderman
Wags with his tar-warm feet;
He puts his boots in the city
Whose own back yard is sweet.

His watch is round as an eyeball
And quick inside as an eye;
On the warm tar swell of his stomach
It ticks his hours by.

Away they go like the children
And the innocent darkness creeps
Among the wires and windows;
The alderman nods and sleeps.

God bless the alderman's stomach
And bless his good gray heart,
Keep him from bugs and goblins
And from things that go bump, apart!

50

A HAPPY GHOST

As though he'd overslept he died
And when he did he filled the room
With the dampness of his pride
Like the smell of bloom in hothouses

Wherein are growing many droopy plants:
A palm tree, a banana tree and ferns,
Orchids and other petal skins, and toads.

Meanwhile his little ghost infects the roads,
A happy ghost, whom everything enchants,
Bedded not yet among the bones and urns.

DOMESTIC

A man should build himself a house and put himself inside
And fill it full of furniture, and get himself a bride
To fill it full of cooking smells and pickle smells and wit
And all in pleasure breed it full and make a nest of it.

It won't work I've asked around although it sounds so nice
   Miss
Belaney and Miss Decharmes and Dorothy say no dice.

51

ESCAPE

Fleeing from Mrs. McGonigle, Mr. Smith
Took refuge in a public telephone booth
Whence he rang, as he always did, forthwith,
The gospel tabernacle, home of Truth.

Mrs. McGonigle meanwhile searched the streets
Asking herself as she did so why she did.
His life with her she knew was a nest of sweets
From which he beat it, now and again, and hid.

And every time he ended up on his knees
Among his burning friends at Gospel Hall
Who put his soul through fire and gave it ease
With balm from the Apostles, especially Paul.

These were his most exciting days, no doubt,
Groaning and urging a consciousness of sin,
But Mrs. McGonigle always found him out
Sooner or later, and motherly gathered him in.

Truly a man is never lonely here
And least of all at the moment of wild escape
In the telephone booth, a moment of bliss and fear
Between this world and the next, between fire and rape.

MRS. McGONIGLE ON DECORUM

Don't be nervous, Mary Anne,
   Don't be nervous, dear!
Carry a little water can
   To catch the quiet tear.

Don't let anyone see it there,
   Don't let anyone know;
Put it away in your clothes somewhere,
   Dump it before you go!

Do as the lovely ladies do,
   Mark the words of the gents,
Don't run off when you're spoken to,
   Don't start arguments!

Ah, that my hours beside the sink
   Were printed in a book!
Many who tremble on the brink
   Would take a second look.

Don't be nervous, Mary Anne,
   Everyone else, you know,
Carries a little water can
   And doesn't let it show.

53

LIFE FROM A GOLDFISH BOWL

Mr. Murple called upon his mother
Bringing a bottle of gin for Mother's Day;
They tolerate, indeed they love each other
And often rub each other the right way.
'Mother,' he said, 'I brought you this here gin,
Product of Messrs. Moult, Moultville, you know.
Look at the fancy piece of glass it's in!
Times have been extra good to Moult and Co.'

'Drat the flies, they're awful bad this year!'
She said, waving a big one from her nose.
'What have you got there? Bless your heart, my dear!
Put it on the piano, by the rose.
A nice red rose to show I'm still alive:
Fifty cents they asked me for it, thieves!
Yellow to show you're dead is fifty-five
All done up in ferny things and leaves.'

What a life for a goldfish, day and night
Who fins in Mr. Murple's mother's bowl!
He gets a bit of flat stuff for a bite
Maybe, or maybe ant eggs—eaten whole—
And notes the goings-on with goggle face
Of all the world around about in air:
Of Mr. Murple with his gloves and grace
Coming with gifts for mother in her lair.

FLOWERS AND CHILDREN

Mrs. Beleek, an aunt of ours,
Lifts her behind among her flowers
Putting ingenious stuff around
To baffle bugs and coax the ground.

What does she think about all day?
Children, that's what, that come her way:
Bobby, Ronald, Elizabeth-Anne,
Pie-faced Linda and sweet Diane.

Little Diane, to cite a case:
What a pleasure to, well, erase!
And Linda, how bumpable-off, with skill,
Over the bathroom window sill.

From any corner around the lot
Neatly a hopeful might be shot,
Neatly to bite the bordered dust
Treated for fungus rot and crust.

Heaven visits on Aunt Beleek
Every once or twice a week
Moments almost too bright to bear.
Bless her old heart, she should take care!

THE HERO'S KITCHEN

A seal of holiness descends
    Upon the kitchen floor;
Mrs. Belaney and her friends
    Knit and discuss the war.
Mrs. Belaney has a son
    —Had, I should say, perhaps—
Who deeds of gallantry has done,
    Him and some other chaps.

Into his hand the Seraphim
    Gave the destructive sword,
Beckoning as they did in him
    Creation's restless lord.
Fire and blood became his trade;
    Gentle and clumsy one
At home he was, but on parade
    Creation's restless son.

Mrs. Belaney feels the wall
    Rustle with angel wings;
Tears of a sacred nature fall
    Into the knitting things.
Then begins tea, and cakes and pies
    Muffle the ladies' chat;
Out of the shadows angel eyes
    Watch the encroaching fat.

THREE QUESTIONS

Mr. Murple has three questions to ask
But never remembers the order in which they come.
First, he says, is there anything under the mask?
But no, that's wrong! And he starts to count at his thumb.

Something about the soul I know is one,
And something to do with space is another, I think;
As for the third, it has never even begun
That anyone's heard. I've filled his head with drink,

Very good drink too: whisky, and anisette,
And Van der Hum, and rum to open his brain
But, Wait a minute, that's wrong! is all I get.
Yet one of his questions is crucial I know. The strain

Is awful. I wish it would end some way!
Nobody knows what's coming, but somebody cares—
His mother cares and so do I, all day,
God knows we hardly stop to say our prayers.

THE DUFUFLU BIRD

The call of the dufuflu bird
 For which I have an ear
Falls like the uncreating word,
 But only some can hear.

And often at the droop of day
 When evening grumbles in
The great dufuflu has his say
 Above the traffic's din

All unattended save by me
 And by a special few
Who hear his awful summons; we
 Attend its meaning too,

We, maybe, when we're on a walk
 And maybe feeling low
Hear his apocalyptic squawk
 And think it's time to go.

Our hearts respond, our souls respond,
   The very we of us
Takes off, as one might say, beyond,
   But then comes back, alas!

We hardly fuss, perhaps we pray
   —The timid drop a tear—
And go our uncomplaining way
   Keeping a watchful ear

For when the great dufuflu bird
   May open up again
In such a voice as will be heard
   By us and all good men.

MR. GOOM

Earth fills her lap for Mr. Goom
With gifts, of which in studied measure
And with the savoir-faire of doom
He makes selection for his pleasure.

Yet life is often very sad
For Mr. Goom, he doesn't know
Whether it's really good or bad
Its sweetest moments sour so.

And though he cherishes his gifts
—His lovely clothes, his lovely friends—
His dilettante attention shifts
From time to time to mortal ends

And then he finds he needs a drink
Or else a Turkish bath to chase
His apperception from the brink
Of darkness to a brighter place.

Always around the door he knows
The brink of darkness drops away
And sure enough the door will close
After him over it one day.

The tears I shed for Mr. Goom
Are soft in character and fine
As his own amiable perfume:
They fall between his fate and mine.

PASTORALE

The grasshopper does not so free
The silly summer time dispense
As Mr. Murple in a tree
Playing upon wind instruments.

He fills the air with ornaments
Trilling and running gracefully
Oblivious of audience
And in his improvising free.

The snake, the frog, the bumblebee
And other forest residents
Hark to his music solemnly
Soothed to a charming diffidence.

Part Three
IN IT

IN IT

The world is a boat and I'm in it
Going like hell with the breeze;
Important people are in it as well
Going with me and the breeze like hell—
It's a kind of a race and we'll win it.
Out of our way, gods, please!

The world is a game and I'm in it
For the little I have, no less;
Important people are in it for more,
They watch the wheel, I watch the door.
Who was the first to begin it?
Nobody knows, but we guess.

The world is a pond and I'm in it,
In it up to my neck;
Important people are in it too,
It's deeper than this, if we only knew;
Under we go, any minute—
A swirl, some bubbles, a fleck. . . .

THIS WAY DOWN

How do I know the time by looking at the clock?
How do I know there's trouble by hearing people talk?
How do I go to heaven? The world is wrapped in air.
This way down to the bottom the signs and maps declare.

Is there a proper bottom? I tell my courage so.
God in His mercy made one where timid people go.
Satan sits on the bottom—on his—and wags his eye;
The world gives way toward him; what can I do but fly?

Nightly the lonely diesel that mourns among the fields
Calls to me in my bedroom till my compassion yields;
Nightly the wee jet aircraft that search the dreadful sky
Draw the tears to my pillow that has so long been dry.

My room is floored with pity, my walls are shored with grief,
My roof is wide to Heaven, my door invites the thief;
Why am I not then airborne? They mock me, night and day,
The clock and the blundering diesel and the wee jets far away.

WET

It's rained sort of day after day
Till the bottom is, as it were, wet;
My feelings are all washed away
But something is left of me yet

And whatever the something may be
I take it to eat and to bed
Because after all it's still me—
Come rain, wash the lot. Let's be dead.

YEATS' GHOST

The ghost of Mr. Yeats
Visited us the other night
While we were in the Bogeyman Club
Beering by candle light.

He looked at the lovely glasses,
Tall as queens of the Sidhe, and bright:
Mind if I take a sniff? he said,
It is a ghost's right.

SMILERS

After me the smilers come
Put their comforts everywhere
Which I'm helpless to be from,
Smile to death the prosperous air.

Smile to death my dearest one,
Put their comforts on her knee;
Love has gifts for everyone,
Don't be shedding tears for me!

After all, I made some dough,
By and by I made some more;
Anywhere I like to go
Friends, my goodness, friends galore!

From the bottom of the street
Where we'll all at last do well
Comes a fellow smiler's bleat
And a sulphur kind of smell.

EATING FISH

Here is how I eat a fish
   —Boiled, baked or fried—
Separate him in the dish,
   Put his bones aside.

Lemon juice and chive enough
   Just to give him grace,
Make of his peculiar stuff
   My peculiar race.

Through the Travellers' Hotel
   From the sizzling pan
Comes the ancient fishy smell
   Permeating man.

May he be a cannier chap
   Altered into me,
Eye the squirming hook, and trap,
   Choose the squirming sea.

MAIL-ORDER CATALOGUE

A paper land where death don't seem to come,
Where flannelette pyjamas, wreathed in smiles,
And ladies' corsets, smug as chewing gum,
Dwell overleaf from remedies for piles;

Where medicines to keep the stork at bay
—Flushed in the gents' long woollen underwear—
Offer themselves as well to passion's prey
As to the fruitful housewife, taking care.

Music of hi- and medium-fi degree,
Sump pumps, rubber gloves, and tires,
Castrators, bottle-warmers, lingerie,
Everything heart demands, or hand requires.

In spring and fall, when serious young men
Comfort themselves that all that lives must die,
Tax and the teeming catalogue again
Come round, and give mortality the lie.

A LITTLE LIGHT

A little creeping light
Creeps about in the night

Hunts in the huge dark
A little room for a spark.

The dark is without surprise
It knows by a thousand eyes

Eyes without body or breath
And always there, like death,

Watching the upstart light
Hunt its place in the night.

O EARTH, TURN!

The little blessed Earth that turns
Does so on its own concerns
As though it weren't my home at all;
It turns me winter, summer, fall
Without a thought of me.

I love the slightly flattened sphere,
Its restless, wrinkled crust's my here,
Its slightly wobbling spin's my now
But not my why and not my how:
My why and how are me.